ILLUSTRATED BY
JESSICA HOFFMANN DAVIS

Jacks
and
Jack Games:

Follow My
Fancy

MARTA WEIGLE

DOVER PUBLICATIONS, INC.
NEW YORK

Published in Canada by General Publishing Company, Ltd., 30 Lesmill Road, Don Mills, Toronto,
Ontario.
Published in the United Kingdom by Constable
and Company, Ltd., 10 Orange Street, London WC 2.

Jacks and Jack Games: Follow My Fancy is a new
work, first published by Dover Publications, Inc., in
1970.

International Standard Book Number: 0-486-22081-8
Library of Congress Catalog Card Number: 71-81735

Manufactured in the United States of America
Dover Publications, Inc.
180 Varick Street
New York, N. Y. 10014

Preface

WHEN I went to camp, my friends and I played jacks in our spare time. The rules were as free or as strict as we wished. In general, the rules and fancies I have included in this book are the ones we used. They are not "official"; they are not complete. You can always make up new ones or change the ones given. The fancies in this book are of varying degrees of difficulty and provide many games for novices, intermediates, and experts.

Read this book carefully. Follow the instructions. And—have fun! Jacks are fun!

Contents

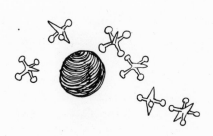

Introduction

PEOPLE have played some form of jacks since ancient times, when they used bones, stones, seeds, or small filled cloth bags, instead of the little metal or plastic six-pronged objects in use today. Each player threw five or more of these counters into the air and tried to catch them in his hand or on the back of it. Every one he missed counted against him. Sometimes players threw another seed or stone or a larger bone up into the air while they picked up the ones they missed, just as we toss up a ball today. Evidence of such games, which are also called Dibs or Knucklebones, has been found on jars from ancient Greece, in records from Roman times, and even in prehistoric caves.

Games very similar to these old ones are played all over the world even today.

In *Czechoslovakia*, six seeds are tossed into the air and caught in the hand or on the back of it. This is done with the right and then the left hand. Every uncaught seed counts against the player.

In *Egypt*, the players start with about ten apricot seeds. One person takes all the seeds, throws them up, and tries to catch them on the back of his hand. The number of seeds he catches determines how many turns he gets. He then throws all the seeds out on the ground. He picks up one, throws it up into the air and gathers as many seeds as he can from those on the ground before catching the falling seed. He repeats this until he has used up his turns. The player who gathers the most seeds wins.

In *Japan* and *China*, a player drops cloth bags filled with beans, rice, or sand onto a table. He picks up one and throws it into the air, and tries to pick up as many bags as possible from the table before catching the falling bag. Each time he throws the bag up, he tries to keep all the bags he has already gathered in one of his hands.

Most of these games involve winning more counters than anyone else.

The modern game of jacks requires much more skill than these early variations. We now use small, six-pronged metal objects called "jacks" (the name *jack* comes from an old word meaning "men") and usually also a small rubber ball. The game is built around a single basic or "plain" move, in which a player throws the ball up into the air, picks up from one to six jacks, and then catches the ball before it bounces more than once. Every game starts with *plainsies*, a series of "plain" moves in which a player picks up first one jack, then two at a time, then three, and so on, and finally all six in time to catch the ball before the second bounce (see p. 10). Next, each player must do some form of *backsies*, in which procedures are reversed (described on p. 12). Then the excitement begins as players choose different variations of the "plain" moves of throwing, picking up, and catching the jacks. These variations are called *fancies*, and they are described in detail in Part Two of this book (p. 21).

Fancies may be as simple as Plainsie Double Bouncies, in which the player lets the ball bounce twice before catching it; as complicated as King Cobra (p. 62), in which the plain move is followed by throwing both jacks and ball into the air and catching the jacks with a downward motion of one hand, and the ball with a downward motion of the other; or as difficult as Quadruple Everlastings (p. 83), a special variation which the player must complete without making a single mistake. The player who wins at plainsies and backsies usually *chooses* the fancies which his opponents must follow, and tries to make it as difficult as possible for them to overtake and pass him. Of course, not all games are stiff battles; players may decide before they start that they wish to relax the rules and play the game *funsies* rather than *strictsies* (see p. 14). In every case, the player who is farthest ahead when the game ends wins.

Throughout this book instructions are worded on the assumption that the reader is right-handed. Left-handed readers should reverse directions for right and left hands.

As the fancies become more and more difficult, players must be more and more skillful. However, if you read this book carefully and practice diligently, you should be able to develop good skills and play a championship game.

PART ONE

Fundamentals

I · Preparations for Play

YOU NEED a ball, six to ten jacks, a smooth surface, and two or more people to play jacks. (This book is written for games involving six jacks. It is best to start out with six jacks, especially if your hands are small. When your fingers are longer and when you become more skillful, you will be able to play most of the fancies with ten jacks if you wish.)

Ball: A jack ball is a small rubber ball about $1\frac{1}{4}$ inches in diameter. To test a ball, toss it several feet straight up in the air. A good ball will bounce straight back up at least half as high as it falls. If you have a choice of balls, select the one that bounces the highest and straightest.

Jacks: Jacks are six-pronged metal objects; each prong is about $\frac{3}{8}$ of an inch long. Heavy, thick jacks do not spin easily and tend to stay together better when you throw or flip them, and therefore are generally considered to be the best. However, if your hands are very small, it may be wise to start with lighter, thinner jacks.

Smooth surface: One has more control over the jacks when he plays on the floor, rather than on a table or other elevated surface. Floors that are smooth but not highly polished make the best playing surfaces, because jacks slide and slip too easily on a highly polished floor. Wood floors are all right if they do not have splinters in them or large cracks between the boards. Tile floors with a dull finish are very good. Be sure to allow at least three square feet of playing space.

Players: Any number of people can play jacks. When one player misses, the next player takes the ball and jacks and plays until he misses. Two or three players usually have a more exciting game than a larger number of players because everyone gets his turn sooner. Don't forget, of course, that you can always play by yourself to practice fancies and techniques. You can also set a time limit and see how far you get before the time runs out.

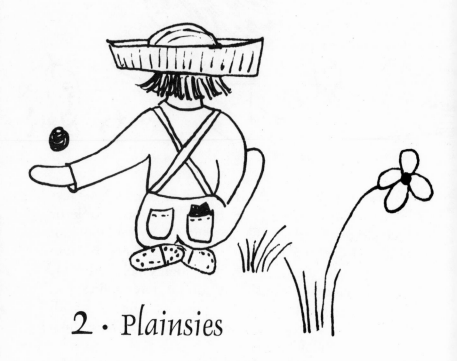

2 · Plainsies

PLAINSIES, the basic or regular jack game, consists of flipping, throwing out the jacks, and picking them up in various combinations before the ball bounces more than once.

You can flip with one or two hands. In two-handed flipping, first cup your hands together so that the little fingers are touching. Shake the jacks around between your hands until they fall into a compact line or row. Then throw the jacks straight into the air and catch them on the back of your hands. To do this, make a trough by holding your hands with the thumbs together and the index fingers touching each other. Turn the backs of your hands up so there is less chance for the jacks to fall out of the trough. When you catch the jacks in the trough, jiggle them a moment to get them together again and throw them into the air. Then catch them with your hands cupped in the original position to complete the flip.

One-handed flipping is harder than two-handed flipping. Jiggle the jacks around on the palm of one hand until they are in a compact row. Then toss them straight up into the air and catch them on the back of your hand between your fingers. You will catch more jacks if you extend your fingers and bend them back slightly. Allow a very small space between the fingers; a prong of a flipped jack will fall into one of these spaces, thus preventing the jack from falling off your hand. Do not try to catch the jacks directly on the back of your hand because they will usually bounce off. Then toss the jacks into the air again and catch them in your palm to complete the flip. You are not permitted to use your free hand to arrange the jacks during a one-handed flip.

Whether you use one or two hands, a flip is incomplete until you have thrown and caught the jacks twice—once on the back of your hand (or hands) and once in the palm. Thus, the word "flip," wherever it is used in this book, means that you throw the jacks and catch them both ways.

In the beginning of a game, players take turns flipping. Whoever catches the most jacks goes first. If there is a tie, take turns flipping until it is broken.

The person who is to start now takes the jacks and flips again. This is the first step in *plainsie onesies* (see below). If he catches all the jacks on the backs of his hands and again on the palms, he has completed onesies and flips again for *twosies*. If he catches all the jacks a second time, he may go on and flip for *threesies*. It is possible to flip all the way through *sixies*. However, when he misses a jack, he must put the jacks he has caught into his left hand and begin playing from where he missed in flipping, be it onesies, twosies, threesies, or any other.

If a player drops any of the jacks when flipping for onesies (or twosies, etc.), the game will proceed as follows:

Onesies: Keep the jacks you have caught in the flip in your left hand, and leave the fallen jacks (or jack) where they dropped on the playing surface. With your right hand, throw the ball about a foot or so straight up into the air. Then with the same (right) hand, pick up one of the jacks that dropped out during your flip. Next, catch the ball in your right hand before it bounces more than once. Now put the jack you have just picked up in your left hand. Continue this procedure until all the jacks have been picked up and put into your left hand.

Twosies: Throw out all the jacks onto the floor. Follow the instructions given for onesies, but this time pick up *two* jacks at a time (until they are all picked up).

Threesies: Pick up three jacks at a time.

Foursies: Pick up four jacks, then two jacks.

Fivesies: Pick up five jacks, then one jack.

Sixies: Pick up all six jacks.

You can keep playing until you miss.

There are ten basic "fouls" that count as "misses"

in almost all the plainsies and fancies described in this book. These are as follows:

1. *Not beginning at the place where you missed during your last turn.* When it is your turn, you must start with the number and fancy on which you missed during your last turn.
2. *Changing your position after the jacks are thrown out.* You may not move around in order to sit on a different side of the thrown jacks.
3. *Moving a jack as you pick up one near it.* You must not move any jack but those which you are picking up.
4. *Trying for the same jack more than once.* You may try to pick up a jack or jacks only once.
5. *Picking up the wrong number of jacks.* You must pick up the *number* of jacks called for at each level, *i.e.,* onesies, twosies, threesies, and so on.
6. *Using help to catch the ball.* You may not use your clothes or any part of your body to help you catch the ball. Using two hands to catch the ball also counts as a miss.
7. *Letting the ball bounce more than once, or not letting it bounce at all.* Unless you are playing a special fancy, the ball must bounce once, and only once, before you catch it. (Some of the fancies described in Part Two of this book call for different numbers of bounces.)
8. *Using the wrong hands for jacks or ball.* Unless you are doing a special fancy, you must pick up the jacks with the same hand with which you catch the ball.
9. *Dropping the ball or jacks.* It counts as a miss if you drop the ball or any of the jacks before you put the jacks you have just picked up into your other hand.

10. *Arranging the jacks.* You cannot arrange the jacks after they have been thrown out or when they are in your right hand.

In plainsies (or in any fancy), if you miss before you get through threesies, you must begin again on onesies.

When a player gets through sixies, he then starts on a *backsie* of the regular game. The first player to get through plainsie sixies decides which kind of *backsies* the other players must do. There are two kinds:

Plainsie backsies: Just reverse the procedure for plainsies. Throw out all the jacks and do, first, sixies, then fivesies, foursies, threesies, twosies, and finally onesies. *You must not flip for plainsie backsies.*

Easy backsies: Throw out six jacks; pick up five jacks. Throw out the five jacks and pick up four. Never pick up a jack that has already been left on the floor. (For example, if you pick up five and leave one, never touch that one jack again, or it counts as a miss.) Repeat this procedure until all the jacks have been thrown out onto the floor. Now pick up all six jacks.

Plainsies and one kind of backsies are the start of any jack game. After these, the player who has finished them first decides which *fancies* the other players must do. (The procedure for fancies is described in Chapter Five in Part Two of this book.) If a time limit has been set on the game, however, the person who is ahead when the time runs out wins. Players may also decide to play a specific number of fancies. In this case, the person to complete that number first is the winner.

3 . Strictsies and Funsies

THE BASIC game of jacks can be made easier or more difficult, depending on the skill of the players and their inclinations. Easy games are known as *funsies*, difficult ones are called *strictsies*. Here are twelve ways in which to adjust the game to the degree of complexity you want.

To make the game easier:

Overs: If you do not like the way you threw the jacks, you can call "Overs!" and throw them out again.

Cracksies: This situation applies only when playing on floors which have wide cracks between the boards. If any jacks land with one prong in the crack, you may call "Cracksies!" and move them out to one side of the crack.

Kissies: Two or more jacks which are touching each other are called kissies. The first person to call "Kissies!" gets them. If it is the person who threw the kissies, he picks them up, kisses them, and throws them out again. If it is his opponent, the person who threw the kissies cannot pick them up and throw them out again, and must play them as they fell.

Haystacks: Haystacks occur when two jacks fall so that one jack is on top of the other and does not touch the floor. The first person to call "Haystacks!" gets them. If it is the person who threw the haystacks, he can pick them up, separate them, and place the two jacks anywhere he wishes.

Cart-Before-the-Horse: Cart-Before-the-Horse, or doing things in a different order, occurs only in foursies and fivesies. You call "Cart-Before-the-Horse!" or "Carts!" and pick up two jacks first, then four jacks, or one jack, then five.

Split jack: Split jack occurs when the ball bounces on a jack, and it then goes one way and the jack another so that you cannot catch the ball. You call "Split jack," retrieve the ball, and continue playing.

Interference: Anything which interferes with the bouncing ball may be counted as interference. Rugs,

furniture, and other people are included. You call
"Interference!" and throw the ball up again.

To make the game more difficult:

Late jack: If all the jacks do not drop out of your
hand when you throw, but if one or two drop out a little
after the others, your opponent calls "Late jack!" You
then lose your turn.

Hands: In strictsies, sixies must be thrown so that at
least one jack falls outside the area covered by your out-
stretched hand. If this does not happen, you must throw
them out again or lose your turn, depending upon the
decision of the players.

Touch-Me-Not: If you have thrown the jacks especially close to another player, that player may call
"Touch-Me-Not!" Then, you must not touch your
opponent when you pick up the jacks. However, your
opponent may not *move* and *then* call "Touch-Me-Not!"

Drop jack: If you drop any jacks as you transfer
them to your left hand for safekeeping, it is called "Drop
jack," and counted as a miss. Drop jack occurs only when
the fancy does not involve a special way of putting the
jacks into your left hand.

Spilled beans: If you drop any jacks out of your left
hand as you hold them, it is called "Spilled beans" and
counted as a miss.

Naturally, all games do not have to be "pure"
strictsies or "pure" funsies. Players decide which situations they want to count, and disregard the rest.

4 · Hints and Pointers

THE most important part of a jack game is probably the "throw." Even the best players have trouble if their throwing technique is poor. You will be able to develop your own ways (techniques) of throwing as time goes on, but here are some pointers to help you.

1. *Remember which number (onesies, twosies, etc.) you are on.* If you are on fivesies, do not throw the jacks out as far as you would for twosies. In onesies, twosies, and threesies, the jacks should land farther apart because you must pick up smaller groups at a time. But in foursies and fivesies, they should land more compactly since you must pick them up in larger groups. Naturally, when you have to pick up all six jacks, even if you are playing Hands, you do not want the jacks strewn all over the floor.

2. *Throw the jacks out with the side of your hand touching the floor.* Using this method, you will have the most control over the way the jacks land; they are less likely to splatter when they hit the floor, as they do if you throw them out with the palm of your hand over the floor.

3. *Throw the jacks so that they land somewhat in a line.* The best time to use the "sweeping motion" (described on p. 18) is when the jacks are in a line. To do this, as you throw the jacks out with the side of your hand touching the floor, hold the jacks with your fingers bent lightly around them. Then, with your fingers still slightly bent, throw the jacks out by turning your hand down to the floor so that the thumb side tips over a bit. If this is done, the jacks should roll out more in a line than in a clump.

4. *Use cross-throwing whenever possible.* Cross-throwing can be done when the fancy does not involve transferring all the jacks to the left hand. For example, if you are doing *plainsie foursies*, pick up four jacks first and put them in your left hand. Then pick up the remaining two, but do not put them in your left hand. Instead, throw out the four from your left hand *and* the two from your right hand. This makes it much easier to throw the jacks so that they mingle in groups of three, four, five, or six.

(Use the throwing pointers described in items 2 and 3 above for both hands as you cross-throw.)

Naturally, you may find other throwing techniques which will work better for you. However, if the techniques given here are practiced, they make for consistently better throwing.

After you have thrown the jacks out, the next step is to pick them up easily and quickly, without "missing." Here are some pointers to help you find the best way.

1. *Toss the ball up as high as necessary according to your throw.* If you have thrown the jacks badly and see that you will need more time to pick up the correct number, throw the ball up higher than you usually would.

2. *Control the way you toss the ball up.* Be very careful about the way you toss the ball up. Try to ensure that it will not bounce on a jack or group of jacks. Also, be sure it will not bounce too far away for you to catch it easily. Always keep one eye on the ball so you will have your hand right under it to catch it.

3. *Be very careful with close jacks.* If the jacks have landed very close together, toss the ball up high. You may grab a jack from the side by grasping one prong with your thumb and finger and sliding it carefully away from the jack close to it before you pick it up. If you slide a jack back from another close jack before you pick it up, you will not usually move the other one.

4. *Pick up the jacks with a sweeping motion.* Except in unusual situations, a sweeping motion is the best method for picking up the jacks. Sweep along the floor with your thumb and first finger, the top of your fist, or the side of your hand.

If you use the top of your fist, leave your thumb out along the floor and use it to close on the jacks you pick up. Leave your index finger slightly up so there is more space for the jacks. If you use the side of your hand to sweep, bend your fingers slightly and tip the thumb side of your hand over a little. Draw your fingers around the jacks to pick them up.

The sweeping motion is good for two reasons. You are less likely to miss or drop any of the jacks than if you plucked them from above. You are also able to sweep the jacks away from the ones remaining so they are less likely to be moved.

There are many other tricks and hints for picking up jacks. They vary with each situation. However, there is one hint that is very important:

THINK BEFORE YOU DO ANYTHING: Think how you want the jacks to land before you throw them. Think which jacks you want to pick up before you throw the ball up. Think what you must do with the jacks when you pick them up.

In short, if you practice a lot and concentrate on what you are doing, you will soon be able to work on more difficult fancies.

PART TWO

Fancies

5 · Fancies

WHEN you have mastered plainsies, the regular jack game, and have learned all the rules, you will be ready to use this part of the book.

A *fancy* is a variation of plainsies which usually requires more skill than plainsies does. The first person to get through all of plainsies and one backsie can introduce any fancy he pleases. That is how *fancy* got its name—the player introduces any variation he "fancies" or "wishes" to play.

Introducing fancies: A fancy is introduced by throwing the ball up, slapping the floor, and catching the ball after it bounces once. This is repeated four times. Each time, the player says one line of the following chant:

> First game,
> My fancy,
> Follow my fancy,
> (*name of fancy*).

If the player does not catch the ball after the first bounce, it counts as a "miss." It is also a miss if he gives the wrong name to a fancy. A player can flip for all fancies except Novelties (Chapter 10) and Everlastings (Chapter 12). *All the rules and misses for plainsies apply to fancies.*

Naturally, not all the fancies and possibilities for fancies are included in this book. Only the basic ones and their variations are explained. Following are several ways to *vary* the fancies which are described in the next seven chapters:

Changing hands: You may make a fancy more difficult by reversing the hands and playing with your left hand if you are right-handed, or with your right hand if you are left-handed.

Bounces: The number of times the ball must bounce can be varied to make a fancy harder or easier. No bouncies, double bouncies, and triple bouncies can be added to most fancies.

Backsies: Except for Everlastings, the only fancy which includes backsies, a fancy can be made longer by adding backsies to it.

Everlasting: Because it is possible for your opponent to "flip through" a fancy (*i.e.*, to flip and catch all the jacks six times in a row), he therefore does not actually have to do it at all. For this reason you may decide to make any fancy "everlasting." This means that a player cannot flip for a particular fancy; he must instead throw out all the jacks and begin on onesies. Furthermore, if a player misses before finishing the entire fancy, he must start all over again on onesies. Of course, this is only a means by which a fancy may be *varied*, and should not be confused with the specific fancy, Everlastings.

Ten jacks: All the fancies in this book are written for six jacks. However, most of them can be played with ten, which makes a fancy harder and longer.

Multiple fancies: A *multiple* fancy means that a player must do the *motions* of a fancy two, three, four, five, or even six times, before the ball bounces more than once. Following is an outline for doing the multiple fancies:

Double: When a fancy is doubled, a player must make *two separate motions* to pick up the jacks before catching the ball. For example, in twosies Double Pigs in the Pen (see p. 35) throw the ball up, slide two jacks into the "pen" (your hand), then slide in two more, and catch the ball before it bounces more than once. You must not slide in four jacks at once: slide in two jacks, and then two more *in two separate motions*. Next, slide the remaining two jacks into the pen and *slap the floor* (to replace the second motion, see p. 27). In other words, pick up the jacks according to the following groups:

	FIRST	SECOND	THIRD
ONESIES:	one-one	one-one	one-one
TWOSIES:	two-two	two-slap	
THREESIES:	three-three		
FOURSIES:	four-two		
FIVESIES:	five-one		
SIXIES:	six-slap		

Triple: When a fancy is tripled, you must pick up the jacks *in three separate motions before catching the ball:*

	FIRST	SECOND
ONESIES:	one-one-one	one-one-one
TWOSIES:	two-two-two	
THREESIES:	three-three-slap	
FOURSIES:	four-two-slap	
FIVESIES:	five-one-slap	
SIXIES:	six-slap-slap	

Quadruple: When a fancy is quadrupled, you must pick up the jacks *in four separate motions* before catching the ball:

	FIRST	SECOND
ONESIES:	one-one-one-one	one-one-slap-slap
TWOSIES:	two-two-two-slap	
THREESIES:	three-three-slap-slap	
FOURSIES:	four-two-slap-slap	
FIVESIES:	five-one-slap-slap	
SIXIES:	six-slap-slap-slap	

Quintuple: When a fancy is quintupled, you must pick up the jacks *in five separate motions* before catching the ball:

	FIRST	SECOND
ONESIES:	one-one-one-one-one	one-slap-slap-slap-slap
TWOSIES:	two-two-two-slap-slap	
THREESIES:	three-three-slap-slap-slap	
FOURSIES:	four-two-slap-slap-slap	
FIVESIES:	five-one-slap-slap-slap	
SIXIES:	six-slap-slap-slap-slap	

Sextuple: When a fancy is sextupled, you must pick up the jacks *in six separate motions* before catching the ball:

	FIRST
ONESIES:	one-one-one-one-one-one
TWOSIES:	two-two-two-slap-slap-slap
THREESIES:	three-three-slap-slap-slap-slap
FOURSIES:	four-two-slap-slap-slap-slap
FIVESIES:	five-one-slap-slap-slap-slap
SIXIES:	six-slap-slap-slap-slap-slap

(Sextupled fancies are *almost impossible* to do even with a lot of practice and much skill.)

It counts as a "miss" if you do not pick up the jacks in separate motions or if you slap the floor the wrong number of times.

Every basic fancy has many possible variations. In addition to the above, there are three skills which a player may use in doing the fancies in the chapters in the remainder of this book. These skills may be used as *part* of a basic fancy or as a *variation* of a basic fancy. These three skills are:

Backward flip: After you have picked up the jacks, hold them on your fingers in front of the ball (which is in your palm). Put your thumb over the ball so it will not roll off your hand. Jiggle the jacks so that they clump together. Then, toss them into the air—not too high, for they should stay together—back toward the palm of your hand. While the jacks are in the air, move the ball quickly forward on your hand with your thumb so that the fingers curl over it and hold it. Now catch the jacks in the palm of your hand, using your thumb and palm to form a cup in which to catch them.

Forward flip: A forward flip occurs only *after* a backward flip. It is exactly the reverse of a backward flip. At the end, the ball is held by the thumb on the palm of the hand, and the jacks are caught and held on the fingers.

Slaps: Slaps, or knocks, may be a *part of* a fancy or a way in which to *vary* it. For instance, when a fancy is doubled or tripled (see p. 24), there will be a time when you cannot make two or three motions to pick up the jacks. Therefore, you must slap the floor with your palm or fist as a substitute for each remaining motion before catching the ball.

If a slap is *part of* the fancy, you must slap in the places indicated in the name of the fancy, as well as slapping instead of making the required number of motions as explained above. For example, in fivesies *Slap Triple Pigs in the Pen Slap* (p. 35), throw the ball up, slap the floor with the palm of your hand, slide five jacks into the "pen," slide the remaining jack into the pen, then slap *twice*—once for the third motion in triple and once because the name of the fancy indicates that you must slap afterwards too—and catch the ball. If you slap in the wrong place or if you slap the wrong number of times, it counts as a "miss." (Any fancy can be varied by placing as many slaps as you wish in the indicated places in the name of that fancy.) In every case, however, always slap *before* catching the ball.

For fancies in which the jacks are still in your hand when you must slap (for example, Double Everlastings, p. 83), knock the floor with your knuckles or the side of your fist.

The remaining seven chapters in this book contain about fifty different fancies arranged according to the *basic skills* involved in them. The fancies in each chapter begin with easy ones, and range to more difficult and complex ones. Listed underneath the regular name of the fancy are indications of the basic variations. For example, the heading for Pigs in the Pen looks like this:

PIGS IN THE PEN

Slap Pigs in the Pen *Slap*
Double Pigs in the Pen
Slap Pigs *Slap* Pigs *Slap*
Triple Pigs   Quadruple Pigs
Quintuple Pigs   Sextuple Pigs

The italicized slaps indicate every place where slaps may be inserted. For example, you might make a fancy: *Slap Slap* Pigs in the Pen *Slap* Pigs in the Pen *Slap Slap Slap*.

Likewise, Triple Pigs, Quadruple Pigs, and so on, may be varied with these slaps. In other words, slaps may be added in the same places indicated for Double Pigs in the Pen. Quintuple and sextuple variations are often almost impossible to do, even if you throw the ball very high in the air.

Backward and forward flips are also indicated by italics. These are paired and hyphenated since they cannot be done separately in a variation. For example, *Forward-backward* Satellites (p. 55) means that *after* doing a backward flip, you flip the jacks forward *and* backward, and then finish the fancy. When the forward-backward or backward-forward is in italics, it means that it can be done any number of times in that place in the fancy. Thus, in addition to each basic fancy, there are eight or ten complex variations which you may use in order to make your games harder and more fun.

The best way to use the following chapters of this book is first to choose a set of ten to twenty fancies and learn them well. This set should include several easy ones as well as two or three hard ones. Include a fancy or two from each chapter so that you will be familiar with the skills involved in all the fancies. Practice very hard and read all the instructions and hints carefully. Then, when you have mastered these, choose several other fancies which interest you. Soon you will be able to do most of the fancies in this book. Of course, the games will gradually require more and more skill. The more skills you master, the more fun it is to win!

6 . Farms

BOTH animals and people contribute to doing the hard work involved in the bustling life on a farm. The fancies in this chapter imitate some of the things they do.

RAKING LEAVES

Slap Raking Leaves *Slap*
Double Raking Leaves
Slap Raking *Slap* Raking *Slap*
Triple Raking   Quadruple Raking
Quintuple Raking   Sextuple Raking

The leaves must be "raked" into a "pile" before they can be burned or carted away. Your right hand is the "rake" and the jacks are the "leaves."

For onesies, throw the ball up into the air and slide ("rake") a jack across the floor to a position directly in front of you; this is the "pile." Then, pick up the jack and catch the ball in your right hand before it bounces more than once. Put the jack in your left hand. Repeat this procedure until all the jacks have been picked up and transferred to your left hand. If you forget to "rake" the jacks into a "pile" before picking them up, it counts as a miss. For twosies, throw all the jacks out onto the floor and "rake" in two at a time. Continue in this way through sixies. When you have finished, the lawn will be raked clean.

In Double Raking Leaves, throw the ball up, rake one jack in front of you, and then rake another into the "pile." Then pick up both jacks and catch the ball before it bounces more than once. Continue this procedure through sixies, slapping when necessary. (Follow the charts in Chapter 5, pp. 24–26, for the *multiples* of Raking Leaves.)

WASH DAY

Slap Wash Day *Slap*   Double Wash Day
Slap Wash *Slap* Wash *Slap*
Triple Wash   Quadruple Wash
Quintuple Wash   Sextuple Wash

It is time to "wash" the jacks. Each one must be "scrubbed" two times back and forth across the floor in order to get it perfectly clean.

For onesies, throw the ball up, pick up one jack and rub it back and forth across the floor two times. Then, still holding the jack, catch the ball before it bounces more than once. Put the "scrubbed" jack in your left hand and continue until all the jacks are "scrubbed." (It is considered a miss if you do not scrub the jack back and forth two times before catching the ball.) For twosies, throw out all the jacks and scrub two at a time: then scrub three, and so on. When you have finished sixies, all the jacks will be spanking clean.

In Double Wash Day, throw the ball up, pick up a jack, and "scrub" it back and forth across the floor two times. Keeping the scrubbed jack in your right hand, pick up another jack and scrub them *both* back and forth two times. Then catch the ball before it bounces more than once. Now put both jacks in your left hand and continue this procedure until all the jacks are scrubbed and picked up. Throw them all out and scrub two, then two more, before catching the ball. (Follow the charts for Multiple Fancies in Chapter 5 for slapping instructions.)

CHERRIES IN THE BASKET

Slap Cherries in the Basket *Slap*
Double Cherries in the Basket
Slap Cherries *Slap* Cherries *Slap*
Triple Cherries   Quadruple Cherries
Quintuple Cherries   Sextuple Cherries

When you pick cherries and put them in a basket, be careful they do not miss the basket. The jacks are the "cherries," and you must pick them up off the floor and put them in your left hand, the "basket." If they do not stay in the basket, the cherries will be ruined: it is a miss and you will lose your turn.

For onesies, throw the ball up, pick up a jack, and put it in the "basket" (your left hand). Catch the ball with your right hand before it bounces more than once. Continue until all the jacks are in the basket. Then, for twosies, throw them out from your left hand, and pick them up and put them in the basket two at a time. Continue through sixies until the tree is picked clean.

In Double Cherries in the Basket, throw the ball up, pick up one jack, put it in the "basket"; then pick up another, put it in the basket too, and catch the ball with your right hand before it bounces more than once. Continue through sixies, slapping when necessary for substitute motions, as explained in Chapter 5.

BREAKING EGGS

Slap Breaking Eggs *Slap*
Double Breaking Eggs
Slap Eggs *Slap* Eggs *Slap*
Triple Eggs   Quadruple Eggs
Quintuple Eggs · Sextuple Eggs

You have to "break" a lot of eggs to make a cake. The jacks are the "eggs" and your left hand is the "bowl." If you forget to break one and put it in the bowl shell and all, or if you miss and let one slip down the side of the bowl, you will ruin your cake; it is a miss and you will lose your turn.

For onesies, throw the ball up, pick up one jack, knock it against the floor once, and put it in your left hand, the "bowl." Then, catch the ball with your right hand before it bounces more than once. Continue until all the jacks are in your left hand; then throw them out and begin twosies, *i.e.*, "break" two at a time before putting them in the bowl. Continue through sixies. (It is a miss if you forget to "break the eggs," or if they fall out of your left hand.) When you have finished sixies, all the eggs will be broken and ready to mix in with your cake.

For Double Breaking Eggs, throw the ball up, pick up one jack, knock it against the floor once, and put it in your left hand; then do the same thing with another jack and catch the ball with your right hand before it bounces more than once. Continue through sixies, slapping according to the charts in Chapter 5.

You may want to vary this fancy by knocking the jacks against the floor *more than once* to "break the eggs."

PIGS IN THE PEN

Slap Pigs in the Pen *Slap*
Double Pigs in the Pen
Slap Pigs *Slap* Pigs *Slap*
Triple Pigs   Quadruple Pigs
Quintuple Pigs   Sextuple Pigs

All the pigs are scattered in the woods, and you must "shoo" them into the pen. The jacks are "pigs," and your left hand is the "pen." If you shoo the pigs past the pen, they will run away; it is a miss and you will lose your turn.

First, cup your left hand and put it down with the side of your little finger lying flat on the floor to form the pen. Then, for onesies, throw the ball up, take one jack with your right hand, and slide it into the pen; next, catch the ball with your right hand before it bounces more than once. You can use the thumb of your left hand to close the pen so that the jack will not bounce out. You cannot move the pen, or it counts as a miss. Continue until all the jacks are in the pen; then remove your left hand, throw the ball up, pick up all six jacks and catch the ball with your right hand, before it bounces more than once. Next, throw out all the jacks from your right hand and start on twosies. Continue through sixies. When you have finished, all the pigs will be safely in the "pen."

In Double Pigs in the Pen, slide first one pig into the pen, then slide in another, before catching the ball with your right hand. Repeat this procedure until all the pigs are in the pen. Refer to the Multiple Fancies in Chapter 5 for slapping instructions.

In *funsies*, a jack can be counted as "in the pen" if you can get it in by pivoting your left hand on your little finger. In other words, if by keeping just the tip of your little finger on the floor, you can get a jack that has slid past the pen and *slide* it in, it does not count as a miss. However, in *strictsies*, if you cannot get a jack into the pen with the entire side of your little finger lying flat on the floor, it counts as a miss.

MICE IN THE BARN

Slap Mice in the Barn *Slap*
Double Mice in the Barn
Slap Mice *Slap* Mice *Slap*
Triple Mice   Quadruple Mice
Quintuple Mice   Sextuple Mice

Mice live in holes in barn walls. When they see the cat coming, they scurry to safety inside their holes. In this fancy, you will slide the "mice" (the jacks) to safety through the "hole" in the barn wall.

First, make a semicircle by resting the tips of the thumb and fingers of your left hand on the floor. This makes the "hole" for the "mice" to run through. Then, for onesies, throw the ball up, slide one jack through the hole, and catch the ball in your right hand before it bounces more than once. You must not move your left hand to change the position of the hole. Continue until the jacks have been slid through; remove your left hand, and with your right hand throw the ball up, pick up all the jacks, and catch the ball before it bounces more than once. Now, throw all the jacks out and slide two at a time through the hole, for twosies. Continue through sixies. When you have finished, all the mice will be safely out of the cat's way.

In Double Mice in the Barn, slide first one jack through the hole, then slide through another, and catch the ball with your right hand before it bounces more than once. Use the charts for Multiple Fancies in Chapter 5 for slapping instructions.

BEES IN THE HIVE

Slap Bees in the Hive *Slap*
Double Bees in the Hive   *Slap* Bees *Slap* Bees *Slap*
Triple Bees   Quadruple Bees
Quintuple Bees   Sextuple Bees

A beehive is full of tiny passageways and cubicles. The bees crawl through these passageways making honey and tending eggs. In this fancy your hand is the "hive," and the jacks are the "bees."

First, spread your left hand flat on the floor, palm down, with your fingers and thumb slightly apart. This forms the passageways of the hive. Then, for onesies, throw the ball up, push one jack into any space between your fingers, and catch the ball with your right hand before it bounces more than once. Do not move your left hand. Continue until all the "bees" are in the "hive"; remove your left hand and leave the jacks on the floor, throw the ball up, pick up all the jacks with your right hand and catch the ball before it bounces more than once. For twosies, throw out all the jacks and push two at a time into the hive. In twosies through fivesies, you cannot put more than one set of jacks in any one space between your fingers or it will count as a miss. When you have finished sixies, all the bees will be in the hive for the night.

In Double Bees in the Hive, throw the ball up, push one jack into a space between your fingers, then push another jack into a different space, and catch the ball with your right hand before it bounces more than once. It counts as a miss if you do not push each set of jacks into a different space. Refer to the charts in Chapter 5 for slapping instructions for multiples of Bees in the Hive.

SHEEP OVER THE FENCE

Slap Sheep over the Fence *Slap*
Double Sheep over the Fence
Slap Sheep *Slap* Sheep *Slap*
Triple Sheep   Quadruple Sheep
Quintuple Sheep   Sextuple Sheep

Sometimes you can get to sleep by counting sheep as they jump over a fence. In this fancy, your left hand is the "fence," and the jacks are the "sheep."

First, place your left hand perpendicular to the floor to make the fence. Then, for onesies, throw the ball up, pick up one jack, put it on the other side of your left hand, and catch the ball with your right hand before it bounces more than once. Do not move your left hand. Continue until all the sheep are on the other side of the fence. Remove your left hand, throw the ball up, pick up all six jacks with your right hand, and catch the ball before it bounces more than once. For twosies, throw all the jacks out and put two at a time over the fence. Then continue through sixies. When you have finished, all the sheep will be in another pasture from that in which they started.

In Double Sheep over the Fence, throw the ball up, put one jack on the other side of the fence, then put another jack over, and catch the ball with your right hand before it bounces more than once.
Refer to the charts in Chapter 5
for slapping instructions.

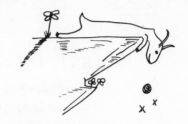

GOATS ON THE MOUNTAIN

Slap Goats on the Mountain *Slap*
Double Goats on the Mountain
Slap Goats *Slap* Goats *Slap*
Triple Goats   Quadruple Goats
Quintuple Goats   Sextuple Goats

Goats love to climb around on the rocks and slopes of mountains. In this fancy, your left hand is the "mountain" and the jacks are the "goats."

First, put your left hand on the floor with your fingers together to form the mountain. Then, for onesies, throw the ball up, pick up one jack and place it on the mountain, and catch the ball with your right hand before it bounces more than once. You may bend your fingers backwards or forwards slightly to make it easier for the jacks to stay on top, but you cannot move your left hand. (If the "goats" fall off the "mountain," it counts as a miss.) Continue playing until all the jacks are on your left hand. Then throw them all out, and begin twosies, *i.e.*, place two jacks at a time on the mountain. At the end of sixies, all goats will be grazing on the mountain.

In Double Goats on the Mountain, throw the ball up, place first one jack on the mountain, then another, and catch the ball with your right hand before it bounces more than once. Continue through sixies, slapping according to the charts in Chapter 5.

CHICKENS IN THE ROOST

Slap Chickens in the Roost *Slap*
Double Chickens in the Roost
Slap Chickens *Slap* Chickens *Slap*
Triple Chickens Quadruple Chickens
Quintuple Chickens Sextuple Chickens

At night, all the chickens settle down in their roost to lay eggs. In this fancy the jacks are the "chickens" and your left hand is the "roost." In the morning, the farmer's wife comes in, and all the chickens scatter from their roosts.

First, hold your left hand about six to ten inches above the floor with the palm down and the fingers spread slightly apart to form the "roost." Then, for onesies, throw the ball up, pick up one jack and place it on the roost in any of the spaces between your fingers, and catch the ball with your right hand before it bounces more than once. Continue until all the chickens have been placed in the roost; then scatter them by spreading wide the fingers of your left hand and allowing the jacks to fall through. For twosies, put two jacks at a time on the roost. At the end of sixies, scatter the jacks from your left hand, throw the ball up, pick up all the jacks with your right hand, and catch the ball before it bounces more than once.

In Double Chickens in the Roost, throw the ball up, put first one jack on the roost, then another, and catch the ball before it bounces more than once. Continue through sixies, slapping when necessary, according to the charts for Multiple Fancies in Chapter 5.

RABBITS DOWN THE HOLE

Slap Rabbits down the Hole *Slap*
Double Rabbits down the Hole
Slap Rabbits *Slap* Rabbits *Slap*
Triple Rabbits
Quadruple Rabbits
Quintuple Rabbits
Sextuple Rabbits

When a rabbit is frightened, he will run and jump down his hole to safety. Here, your left hand forms the "rabbit hole," and the jacks are "rabbits."

First, cup your left hand and put it on the floor with the side of your little finger down. Make a circle by putting the tip of your thumb against the tip of your index finger to form the "hole." Do not move the hole, or it will count as a miss. For onesies, throw the ball up, pick up a jack and drop it down the "hole," and catch the ball with your right hand before it bounces more than once. Continue until all the jacks are "down the hole"; then remove your left hand, throw the ball up, pick up all the jacks with your right hand, and catch the ball before it bounces more than once. For twosies, throw out all the jacks and put two at a time "down the hole." Continue through sixies. When you have finished, every rabbit will be safely in his hole.

In Double Rabbits down the Hole, throw the ball up, pick up one jack and drop it down the hole, then pick up another and drop it down the hole, and catch the ball in your right hand before it bounces more than once. Continue in this way, slapping according to the charts for Multiple Fancies in Chapter 5.

HAY IN THE SILO

Slap Hay in the Silo *Slap*
Double Hay in the Silo
Slap Hay *Slap* Hay *Slap*
Triple Hay   Quadruple Hay
Quintuple Hay   Sextuple Hay

In the summer, the farmer harvests his hay and stores the bundles in the silo for the cows to eat in the winter. Your left hand forms the "silo," and the jacks are the "bundles of hay."

First, put your left fist on the floor with the little finger down. The slight hollow where your thumb wraps around your first finger is the "silo." Do not move your fist, or it counts as a miss. For onesies, throw the ball up, pick up a jack and put it on top of the silo, and catch the ball with your right hand before it bounces more than once. Continue until all the jacks are in the silo; then tip your fist to throw them out again. For twosies, put two jacks at a time in the silo. Continue through sixies. When you have finished, the bundles of hay will be stored in the silo for the coming winter.

In Double Hay in the Silo, throw the ball up, place first one jack in the silo, then another, and catch the ball with your right hand before it bounces more than once. Slaps for multiples of Hay in the Silo are given in Chapter 5.

HANGING TOBACCO

Slap Hanging Tobacco *Slap*
Double Hanging Tobacco
Slap Hanging *Slap* Hanging *Slap*
Triple Hanging
Quadruple Hanging
Quintuple Hanging
Sextuple Hanging

Tobacco must be hung in large barns with slats to dry it before selling. In this fancy, the jacks are the "tobacco bundles," and your left hand is the rafters in the "tobacco barns."

Hold your left hand about ten or twelve inches above the floor with the palm down. For onesies, throw the ball up, pick up a jack and put it in your left hand (closing your fingers over it so that it will not fall out), and catch the ball with your right hand before it bounces more than once. When you "hang" the next bundle of tobacco, be careful that the other bundle (jack) does not fall out, or it will count as a miss. Continue until all the jacks have been picked up; then open your left hand, palm downward, and scatter the jacks. For twosies, hang two bundles at a time. Continue through sixies. When you have finished, the tobacco will be safely hung in the barn to dry.

In Double Hanging Tobacco, throw the ball up, put first one jack in your left hand, then another, and catch the ball before it bounces more than once. Refer to the charts for Multiple Fancies in Chapter 5 for slapping instructions.

7 · Outer Space

SHOOTING stars, flying saucers, and shiny satellites are all part of the far-reaching world of outer space. The fancies in this chapter involve throwing jacks from one hand to another—or, from one planet to another!

SHOOTING STARS

Slap Shooting Stars
Backward-forward Shooting Stars
Slap Backward-forward Shooting Stars
High Shooting Stars
Slap High Shooting Stars
Backward-forward High Shooting Stars
Slap Backward-forward High Shooting Stars

If you look up at the sky on a clear night, you are bound to see several shooting stars streak across the heavens and disappear again. In this fancy, the jacks "shoot" across from your right hand and "disappear" into your left hand.

For onesies, throw the ball up, pick up a jack, and catch the ball with your right hand before it bounces more than once. Next, hold the ball back on the palm of your right hand with your thumb and let the jack remain forward on your fingers. Toss the jack up into the air about six inches and catch it in your left hand. If you do not catch the jack, or if you drop the ball, it counts as a miss. Continue until all the jacks are in your left hand; then throw them all out. For twosies, pick up two at a time and "shoot" them into your left hand. In *Backward-forward* Shooting Stars, do a backward flip, then a forward flip, then shoot the jacks into your left hand.

High Shooting Stars is a more difficult variation of Shooting Stars. Instead of shooting the jacks just six inches or so into the air, you must toss them higher than your head before catching them in your left hand. When throwing the jacks up, throw them so that they *stay together* so that you can catch them without dropping any.

METEORS

Slap Meteors
Backward-forward Meteors
Slap Backward-forward Meteors
High Meteors
Slap High Meteors
Backward-forward High Meteors
Slap Backward-forward High Meteors
Reverse Meteors
Slap Reverse Meteors
Backward-forward Reverse Meteors
Slap Backward-forward Reverse Meteors
High Reverse Meteors
Slap High Reverse Meteors
Backward-forward High Reverse Meteors
Slap Backward-forward High Reverse Meteors

Meteors hit the air surrounding the earth and burst into flame. Sometimes they hit the earth and make a deep crater. In this fancy, the ball is the "flaming meteor" which hits the "earth" (your right hand), and the jacks are the "flames" in its tail which disappear in the "air" (your left hand).

For onesies, throw the ball up, pick up a jack and catch the ball in your right hand before it bounces more than once. Now, holding the jack forward on your fingers and the ball back on your palm, throw both the ball and jack about six inches high into the air. Catch the ball in your right hand and the jack in your left. Continue until all the jacks are in your left hand; then throw them all out and begin twosies. High Meteors is the same as

Meteors, except that you must throw both the ball and the jacks high above your head before catching them. For *Backward-forward* Meteors, first do a backward flip, then a forward flip (p. 27), and then throw the ball and jack into the air.

Reverse Meteors and High Reverse Meteors are exactly like Meteors and High Meteors except that you use the opposite hands for catching the thrown jack and ball. Catch the ball in your left hand and the jack in your right. Then put the jack on the floor beside you and transfer the ball back to your right hand. (This is one of the few fancies in which you do not have to hold the jacks in your left hand.)

FLYING DUTCHMEN

Slap Flying Dutchmen *Slap*   Double Flying Dutchmen
Slap Dutchmen *Slap* Dutchmen *Slap*
Backward-forward Flying Dutchmen
Slap Backward-forward Dutchmen *Slap*
Double *Backward-forward* Flying Dutchmen
Slap B-f Dutchmen *Slap B-f* Dutchmen *Slap*
Reverse Flying Dutchmen   *Slap* Reverse Dutchmen *Slap*
Backward-forward Reverse Flying Dutchmen
Slap Backward-forward Reverse Dutchmen *Slap*

There is an old sea legend about a captain doomed to sail his fully rigged ship forever. The crew is dead, but the captain must sail on eternally because of an oath he once uttered. The ship, called the Flying Dutchman, is often seen by sailors, but they can never come near it. This variation of jacks may have been named Flying Dutchmen because the jacks are always sailing through the air, or possibly because of its elusive goal!

For onesies, throw the ball up, pick up a jack, and catch the ball in your right hand before it bounces more than once. Then, with the jack forward on your fingers and the ball back on your palm, throw both several inches into the air. Catch the jack in your left hand, but let the ball bounce once before you catch it in your right hand. If you drop the jack or ball, or do not catch the ball after one bounce, it counts as a miss. Continue until all the jacks are in your left hand; then throw them all out and do twosies, *i.e.*, sail two "Dutchmen" at a time. *Backward-forward* Flying Dutchmen consists of doing a backward flip, then a forward flip, then "flying the Dutchmen."

Double Flying Dutchmen is much harder than regular Flying Dutchmen. Throw the ball up, pick up a jack, and catch the ball with your right hand before it bounces more than once. Now, with the jack forward on your fingers and the ball back on your palm, throw them both into the air, catching the jack in your left hand. At the same time, with your right hand pick up another jack from the floor and catch the ball before it bounces more than once. Continue this procedure until all the jacks are in your left hand, slapping before you catch the ball if there are no more jacks to pick up. Now start twosies.

Reverse Flying Dutchmen is somewhat different from Flying Dutchmen and Double Flying Dutchmen. First, throw the ball up, pick up a jack, and catch the ball in your right hand before it bounces more than once. Then, throw both the jack and the ball up into the air, catching the jack in your right hand and the ball in your left after it has bounced once. Now, with your *left* hand, throw the ball up, pick up another jack, and catch the ball before it bounces more than once. Next, throw both the ball and jack into the air, catching the ball in your right hand again and the jack in your left. You now have a jack in your left hand and a jack and the ball in your right hand. With your right hand, throw the ball up again, pick up a third jack (thereby making *two* jacks or sets of jacks in your right hand), and catch the ball before it bounces more than once. Repeat until all jacks are in your hands. For twosies, play with two "Dutchmen" at a time, switching hands continually. Remember which hand you should use to catch the ball and which the jacks, because a single mistake counts as a miss.

BLAST OFF

Slap Blast Off *Slap* *Backward-forward* Blast Off
Slap Backward-forward Blast Off *Slap*
Back Blast Off *Slap* Back Blast Off *Slap*
Forward-backward Back Blast Off
Slap Forward-backward Back Blast Off *Slap*

A rocket blasts off from its launching pad by thrusting powerfully against the earth. In this fancy, the ball "blasts off" from the floor while the "launching tower," the jack, falls away into your left hand.

For onesies, throw the ball up, pick up a jack, and catch the ball in your right hand before it bounces more than once. Now, curl your fingers around the jack to secure it, and lightly hold the ball against your palm with your thumb. Turn your hand over with the palm down and throw the ball against the floor. Quickly put the jack in your left hand and catch the ball in your right hand before it bounces again. Continue until all the jacks are in your left hand; then throw them all out and begin twosies. *Backward-forward* Blast Off means doing a backward and a forward flip before "blasting off" the ball.

Back Blast Off has a backward flip *as part of* the fancy. Pick up a jack and do a backward flip. Then, holding the jack against your palm with your thumb and holding the ball lightly with your fingers, turn your palm down and throw the ball against the floor. Quickly put the jack in your left hand and catch the ball in your right hand before it bounces more than once. Continue until all the jacks are in your left hand; then throw them out and begin twosies. *Forward-backward* Back Blast Off means you must flip the jacks backward, forward, and then backward again before "blasting off" the ball.

SHOOT THE MOON

Slap Shoot the Moon
Forward-backward Shoot the Moon
Slap Forward-backward Shoot the Moon
High Shoot the Moon
Slap High Shoot the Moon
High *Forward-backward* Shoot the Moon
Slap High *Forward-backward* Shoot the Moon

Shoot the Moon is an elaboration of Shooting Stars (p. 46). The jacks are "launched" from the palm of your right hand to shoot for the "moon," your left hand.

For onesies, throw the ball up, pick up a jack, and catch the ball in your right hand before it bounces more than once. Then, do a backward flip (p. 27), and, holding the ball forward on your fingers, throw the jack up about six inches into the air and catch it in your left hand. Continue until all the jacks are in your left hand; then throw them all out and begin twosies.

High Shoot the Moon is the same as Shoot the Moon, except that the jacks must be thrown higher than your head before you catch them in your left hand. Be sure you throw them up together in a clump so they will be easier to catch. It is a miss if the person you are playing with thinks the jacks did not go higher than your head.

When adding Forward-backward to this fancy, be sure to do a backward flip first and *then* do as many forward-backward combinations as you wish. Remember, however, that the jacks must always be "launched" from the palm of your hand.

SAUCERS FROM MARS

Slap Saucers from Mars
Forward-backward Saucers from Mars
Slap Forward-backward Saucers
High Saucers from Mars
Slap High Saucers from Mars
High *Forward-backward* Saucers from Mars
Slap High *Forward-backward* Saucers
Reverse Saucers from Mars
Slap Reverse Saucers from Mars
Forward-backward Saucers from Mars
Slap Forward-backward Reverse Saucers
High Reverse Saucers from Mars
Slap High Reverse Saucers from Mars
High *Forward-backward* Reverse Saucers
Slap High *Forward-backward* Reverse Saucers

Saucers from Mars is an elaboration of Meteors (p. 47). The ball is the "red planet Mars," and the jacks are the "flying saucers."

For onesies, throw the ball up, pick up a jack, and catch the ball in your right hand before it bounces more than once. Do a backward flip. Then throw both the ball and the jack up about six inches into the air, catching the ball in your right hand and the jack in your left. Continue until all the jacks are in your left hand; then throw them all out and begin twosies. High Saucers from Mars is the same as regular Saucers, except that you must throw both the jack and the ball high above your head before catching them. *Forward-backward* Saucers from Mars consists of doing first a backward flip (p. 27), and *then* a forward-backward combination or combinations.

In Reverse Saucers from Mars and High Reverse Saucers from Mars, merely reverse the hands you use to catch the jacks and ball in regular Saucers. Catch the jacks in your right hand and the ball in your left. Then put the caught jacks on the floor beside you and transfer the ball back to your right hand. (This is another of the few fancies in which you do not have to hold the jacks in your left hand.)

SATELLITES

Slap Satellites *Slap*
Double Satellites
Slap Satellites *Slap* Satellites *Slap*
Forward-backward Satellites
Slap Forward-backward Satellites *Slap*
Double *Forward-backward* Satellites
Slap F-b Satellites *Slap F-b* Satellites *Slap*
Reverse Satellites
Slap Reverse Satellites *Slap*
Forward-backward Reverse Satellites
Slap Forward-backward Reverse Satellites *Slap*

Satellites is an elaboration of Flying Dutchmen. The "satellite," the jack, has a trial run, falls back again, and is launched as the "earth," the ball, falls away from it.

For onesies, throw the ball up, pick up a jack, and catch the ball in your right hand before it bounces more than once. Now do a backward flip (p. 27) so that the jack rests in the palm of your hand. Then throw the ball and jack up into the air, catching the jack in your left hand and the ball in your right before it bounces more than once. Continue until all the jacks are in your left hand. Then throw them all out and, for twosies, "launch" two satellites at a time. (Be sure to do a backward flip first and *then* do the forward-backward combinations.)

Double Satellites is much harder than regular Satellites. Throw the ball up, pick up a jack, and catch the ball in your right hand before it bounces more than once. Do a backward flip. Then throw both the ball and the jack up into the air, catching the jack in your left hand. At the same time, pick up another jack from the floor with your right hand and catch the ball (in your right hand) before it bounces more than once. Continue this way until all the jacks are in your left hand, slapping before you catch the ball if there are no more jacks to pick up. Then throw all the jacks out and begin twosies.

Reverse Satellites is somewhat different from Satellites and Double Satellites. Throw the ball up, pick up a jack, and catch the ball in your right hand before it bounces more than once. Do a backward flip. Then throw both the ball and jack up into the air, catching the ball in your left hand after it has bounced once and the jack in your right. Now, with your left hand, throw the ball up, pick up another jack, and catch the ball before it bounces more than once. Do a backward flip. Next throw both the jacks and the ball into the air, catching the ball in your right hand again after it has bounced once, and the jacks in your left. You now have a jack in your left hand, and a jack and the ball in your right hand. With your right hand, throw the ball up, pick up a third jack (thereby making *two* jacks or sets of jacks in your right hand), and catch the ball in your right hand before it bounces more than once. Do a backward flip, and repeat the procedure until all the jacks are in your hands. Then, for twosies, throw them all out and play with two "satellites" at a time, being careful to change hands continually. It is important to remember to do the backward flip first, as well as to remember in which hand to catch the jacks and in which the ball, because one tiny mistake will cost you your turn.

8. Cobras

THE cobra is a poisonous Indian snake with a wide hood around its face. He sits with his head up, patiently swaying back and forth while awaiting his prey. Then, with lightning speed, he whips his head down on the animal. In this chapter, you will have to use lightning speed to turn your hands over and "capture" the jacks. If you practice hard, you will be able to "charm" the King Cobra fancy just as the snake charmers in India charm and control the deadly cobras.

BABY COBRA

Slap Baby Cobra
Backward-forward Baby Cobra
Slap Backward-forward Baby Cobra
Back Baby Cobra   *Slap* Back Baby Cobra
Forward-backward Back Baby Cobra
Slap Forward-backward Back Baby Cobra

Baby Cobra is the easiest cobra of all. If you master it first, the others will be much easier to learn.

For onesies, throw the ball up, pick up a jack, and catch the ball in your right hand before it bounces more than once. Now, holding the ball back on the palm of your hand with your thumb, throw the jack a few inches into the air. Catch it by turning your left hand over, palm down, and grab it with a quick downward motion called a "down catch." (Always keep the "captured" jacks in your left hand, even while you are capturing another jack. If you keep your fingers lightly curled around the caught jacks, they will not spill out when you make the next down catch.) Continue until all the jacks have been captured by your left hand; then throw them all out and begin twosies.

Back Baby Cobra is almost exactly like Baby Cobra. The only difference is that you do a backward flip (p. 27) before throwing the jacks into the air, and you hold the ball forward on your fingers instead of on the palm of your hand.

COBRA

Slap Cobra
Backward-forward Cobra
Slap Backward-forward Cobra
Back Cobra   *Slap* Back Cobra
Forward-backward Back Cobra
Slap Forward-backward Back Cobra

In this fancy, there are two cobras, your left hand *and* your right hand, and two objects of prey, the jacks *and* the ball.

For onesies, throw the ball up, pick up a jack, and catch the ball in your right hand before it bounces more than once. Then throw both the jack and ball into the air. "Capture" the jack with a "down catch" of your left hand. Now allow the ball to bounce once, and then "capture" it with a down catch of your right hand to complete the cobra. Continue until all the jacks are in your left hand; then throw them all out and begin twosies.

Back Cobra is almost the same as Cobra, except that it is less difficult. You must do a backward flip (p. 27) before throwing the ball and jacks into the air. Since the jacks are then behind the ball, you are less likely to hit the ball as you try to capture them.

DOUBLE COBRA

Slap Double Cobra
Double *Backward-forward* Cobra
Slap Double *Backward-forward* Cobra
Double Back Cobra
Slap Double Back Cobra
Double Back *Forward-backward* Cobra
Slap Double Back *Forward-backward* Cobra

Double Cobra is a little harder than regular Cobra because the second "cobra," your right hand, must catch the ball *before* it bounces.

For onesies, throw the ball up, pick up a jack, and catch the ball in your right hand before it bounces more than once. Then throw both the jack and the ball up into the air. Now "capture" the jack with a down catch of your left hand and the ball with a down catch of your right hand before it bounces.

Double Back Cobra simply adds a backward flip (p. 27) before throwing the jacks and the ball into the air. It is somewhat harder than Double Cobra because you must capture the ball in front of the jacks before it bounces.

QUEEN COBRA

Slap Queen Cobra
Backward-forward Queen Cobra
Slap Backward-forward Queen Cobra
Back Queen Cobra   *Slap* Back Queen Cobra
Forward-backward Back Queen Cobra
Slap Forward-backward Back Queen Cobra

Queen Cobra is an elaboration of regular Cobra.

For onesies, throw the ball up, pick up a jack, and catch the ball in your right hand before it bounces more than once. Then throw both the jack and the ball up into the air. "Capture" the jack with a down catch of your right hand. Allow the ball to bounce once and capture it with a down catch of your left hand. Now throw the ball up with your left hand, pick up another jack (with your left hand), and catch the ball in the same hand before it bounces more than once. Next, throw both ball and jack into the air, and down catch the jack with your left hand and the ball with your right (which still contains another jack) after it bounces once. Continue in this way until all the jacks are in your hands. Then throw them all out and begin twosies, alternating hands continually.

Back Queen Cobra merely adds a backward flip before throwing the jack and ball into the air. The important thing to remember in these fancies is which hand should "capture" the jacks and which the ball *after* it has bounced once and only once.

KING COBRA

Slap King Cobra
Backward-forward King Cobra
Slap Backward-forward King Cobra
Back King Cobra
Slap Back King Cobra
Forward-backward Back King Cobra
Slap Forward-backward Back King Cobra

King Cobra is an elaboration of Double Cobra (p. 60). It is the hardest cobra of them all!

For onesies, throw the ball up, pick up a jack, and catch the ball in your right hand before it bounces more than once. Then throw both the jack and the ball a few inches up into the air. "Capture" the jack with a down catch of your right hand, and the ball with a down catch of your left *without* allowing it to bounce at all. Now throw the ball up with your left hand, pick up another jack (with your left hand), and catch the ball before it bounces more than once. Next, throw the ball and jack into the air, and capture the jack with a down catch of your left hand and the ball with a down catch of your right (which still contains another jack) *without* allowing it to bounce. Continue until all the jacks are in your hands; then throw them all out and begin twosies.

Back King Cobra follows exactly the same procedure, but adds a backward flip (p. 27) before throwing both the jacks and the ball into the air. Always remember which hand you are going to use. The alternation is very confusing, especially with the added backward flip. Remember, one mistake causes you to lose your turn!

9 . Bugs

On a soft summer evening, the night is alive with a million bugs. The tiny glow of the fireflies lights the lawn. Crickets chirp in the grass. Mosquitoes and gnats buzz around your head. The fancies in this chapter imitate some of the ways to catch anything from a firefly to a housefly.

FIREFLIES

Slap Fireflies
Backward-forward Fireflies
Slap Backward-forward Fireflies

The firefly is the easiest bug to catch. As soon as it turns on its tiny glow, you just close your hand gently around it. In this fancy, you simply let the "fireflies" (the jacks) fall into your hand to "capture" them.

For onesies, throw the ball up, pick up a jack, and catch the ball in your right hand before it bounces more than once. Then, with the jack forward on your fingers and the ball far back on your palm, throw both several inches up into the air. Now move your hand away from the ball (so it will bounce) and at the same time bring it up under the jack to make the catch. Then catch the ball in your right hand before it bounces more than once. Put the jack in your left hand and repeat this procedure until all the jacks are in your left hand. Then throw them all out and begin twosies.

The important thing to remember in Fireflies is to move your hand away from the ball so that it can bounce more easily than it otherwise would. The best way to do this is to move your elbow and lower arm out so that your right hand is almost parallel to your body. In this way, your hand and arm will not obstruct the ball's bounce, and you may capture the jacks quickly—in time to catch the ball before the second bounce.

CRICKETS

Slap Crickets
Backward-forward Crickets
Slap Backward-forward Crickets

It is harder to catch crickets than fireflies. You must slap the ground to make them jump and then grab them.

For onesies, throw the ball up, pick up a jack, and catch the ball in your right hand before it bounces more than once. Then with the ball far back on your palm and the jack forward on your fingers, throw both several inches up into the air. Now move your hand away from the ball so that it can bounce without interference. Then quickly slap the floor with the back of your right hand and bring your hand up under the jack to catch it. Finally, catch the ball in your right hand too before it bounces more than once. Put the jack into your left hand and continue this procedure until all the jacks are in your left hand. Then throw them all out and begin twosies.

If you want to make Crickets harder, you may say it is *strictsie* Crickets. In strictsie Crickets, you must turn your right hand over and slap the floor with your palm instead of with the back of your hand. Then, quickly turn it over again and bring it up under the jack, catching it before capturing the ball.

GNATS

Slap Gnats
Backward-forward Gnats
Slap Backward-forward Gnats

Gnats are so tiny that they are very hard to catch. If you are not quick and accurate, they will keep buzzing around and around your head. In this fancy, if you are not fast and accurate, the "gnats" (the jacks) will elude you and you will lose your turn.

For onesies, throw the ball up, pick up a jack, and catch the ball in your right hand before it bounces more than once. Then, with the jack forward on your fingers and the ball far back on your palm, throw both several inches up into the air. Quickly bring your right hand *over* the ball with a "down catch" (described on p. 58) and "capture" the jack. Then, also catch the ball in your right hand before it bounces more than once. Put the jack into your left hand and continue until all the jacks are in your left hand. Then throw them all out and begin twosies.

In Gnats, it is a good idea to throw the jacks a little higher than the ball so that you are less likely to hit the ball as you make the down catch of the jacks. Also, do not let your hand come down too far on the down catch or you will knock the ball aside.

FLYING ANTS

Slap Flying Ants
Forward-backward Flying Ants
Slap Forward-backward Flying Ants

Flying ants are fairly simple to catch. Wait for them to take a jump and then bring your hand up under them.

For onesies, throw the ball up, pick up a jack, and catch the ball in your right hand before it bounces more than once. Do a backward flip (p. 27). Then with the ball forward on your fingers and the jack far back on your palm, throw both several inches up into the air. Bring your right hand under the jack to catch it. Allow the ball to bounce once and then catch it in your right hand also. Put the jack in your left hand and continue this procedure until all the jacks are in your left hand. Then throw them all out and begin twosies.

Flying Ants is one of the simpler bug fancies because it is easy to move your right hand out of the way of the bouncing ball.

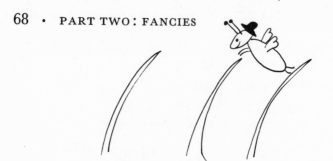

GRASSHOPPERS

Slap Grasshoppers
Forward-backward Grasshoppers
Slap Forward-backward Grasshoppers

Grasshoppers are hard to catch. You have to hit the ground and then be ready to grab them (the jacks) quickly.

For onesies, throw the ball up, pick up a jack, and catch the ball in your right hand before it bounces more than once. Do a backward flip (p. 27). Then with the ball forward on your fingers and the jack back on your palm, throw both several inches up into the air. Knock the floor with the back of your right hand and then bring it up under the jack to catch it. Catch the ball in your right hand too before it bounces more than once. Put the jack into your left hand and continue in this way until all the jacks are in your left hand. Then throw them all out and begin twosies.

Strictsie Grasshoppers is more difficult to do. Instead of knocking the floor with the back of your hand, you must turn your hand over and slap the floor with your palm. Then, turn the palm up again, and bring your hand under the jack to catch it before catching the ball after its first bounce.

MOSQUITOES

Slap Mosquitoes
Forward-backward Mosquitoes
Slap Forward-backward Mosquitoes

Slapping mosquitoes all night is one of the most unpleasant parts of a camping trip. In this fancy, you slap the "mosquito" (the jack) when it is close to you.

For onesies, throw the ball up, pick up a jack, and catch the ball in your right hand before it bounces more than once. Do a backward flip (p. 27). Now, with the ball forward on your fingers and the jack held back on your palm, throw both several inches up into the air. Quickly bring your right hand over the jack and "capture" it with a down catch (described, p. 58). Then catch the ball in your right hand too before it bounces more than once. Put the jack in your left hand and continue in this way until all the jacks are in your left hand. Then throw them all out and begin twosies.

Mosquitoes is not as hard as Gnats (p. 66) because you are less likely to hit the ball with your down catch. However, on the down catch be careful that you do not hit the jacks and splatter them.

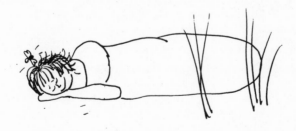

FLIES

Slap Flies
Forward-backward Flies
Slap Forward-backward Flies

Houseflies are the hardest bugs to catch. They are always alert to any movement near them, and they fly away at a moment's notice.

For onesies, throw the ball up, pick up a jack, and catch the ball in your right hand before it bounces more than once. Do a backward flip (p. 27). Then with the ball forward on your fingers and the jack held back on your palm, throw both several inches up into the air. Bring your right hand around so that it is perpendicular to the floor, and, with a side motion, quickly move your right hand in a path parallel to the floor and grab the jack. Then catch the ball in your right hand also before it bounces more than once. Put the jack in your left hand and continue in this way until all the jacks are in your left hand. Then throw them all out and begin twosies.

IO · Novelties

THE fancies in this chapter do not involve a special set of related skills like the fancies in the other chapters. They are all different. Most of them use novel methods for moving and picking up the jacks, like Sweep the Parlor and Jack Be Nimble. They are an interesting change from the longer, more difficult fancies in the other chapters.

ROUND-THE-WORLD

Slap Round-the-World *Slap*

Round-the-World is an elaboration of *plainsies*. For onesies, throw the ball up and pick up a jack. Before you catch the ball again, go "around the world," *i.e.*, bring your hand over and around the ball, catching it from underneath. The best way to do this is to pick up a jack with your right hand from the left side of the ball. Then bring your hand up and over the ball clockwise, ending up right underneath the ball (at six o'clock) to catch it. (Sometimes you may wish to throw the ball higher to give you more time.) Put the jack in your left hand and continue this procedure until all the jacks are picked up. Then throw them all out and begin twosies.

There are two possible places for slaps in Round-the-World. The first is to slap *before* you pick up the jack. The second is to slap *after* you go "around the world" and *before* you catch the ball. You can do this most easily by quickly knocking the back of your hand against the floor. That way, your hand will be ready to open and catch the falling ball.

JACK BE NIMBLE

Double Jack Be Nimble
Triple Jack Be Nimble
Quadruple Jack Be Nimble

This fancy is based on the nursery rhyme about Jack jumping over the candlestick.

Arrange all the jacks in a straight line about two inches apart from one another. Moving from left to right, throw the ball up and lightly brush two fingers through the space between the first two jacks while you say, "Jack be nimble." Then, catch the ball in your right hand before it bounces more than once. (It does not matter which fingers you use to brush, but the third and fourth ones usually are best.) Next, throw the ball up again, lightly brush two fingers through the space between the second and third jacks while you say, "Jack be quick"; then catch the ball before it bounces more than once. Now throw the ball up, pick up the third jack, put it down on the right side of the fourth jack while you say, "Jack jump over...," then catch the ball before it bounces more than once. Finally, throw the ball up, pick up the fourth jack (the one you just jumped) as you say, "... the candlestick," and then catch the ball before it bounces more than once. Put the jack you picked up into your left hand and continue playing in this way until all the jacks have been picked up. As you play, it will become harder and harder to tell which jack to jump because you may have to put a jack from the right end of the line on the right side of the jack on the left end of the line. The space after the jack at the right end of the line counts as the space between that jack and the one at the beginning (left end) of the line. If you move a jack, if you forget to say a line of the rhyme, or say the wrong one, or if you jump the wrong jack, it counts as a miss. Following is an outline of what happens between the time you throw the ball up and the time you catch it before it has bounced more than once:

SAY:	DO:
1) *Jack be nimble*	Brush lightly through the space between the first two jacks.
2) *Jack be quick*	Brush lightly through the space between the second and third jacks.
3) *Jack jump over*	Place the third jack on the right side of the fourth jack.
4) *the candlestick*	Pick up the fourth jack.

In Double Jack Be Nimble, do steps 1) and 2) before catching the ball, then do steps 3) and 4). In Triple Jack Be Nimble, do steps 1), 2) and 3) before catching the ball, then do step 4) and slap twice. For Quadruple Jack Be Nimble, do all four steps before catching the ball!

SWEEP THE PARLOR

Double Sweep the Parlor
Triple Sweep the Parlor
Quadruple Sweep the Parlor

Sweep the Parlor is another fancy with a special layout and a special rhyme. Arrange the jacks according to the diagram on p. 77, with the corner jacks of the square about a foot apart and the remaining jacks clustered in the center. The corner jacks are "chairs," the spaces between them are the "parlor walls," and the center jacks the "dust pile."

With each move, you must say a different line of the rhyme, throw the ball up, do the proper action, and catch the ball before it bounces more than once. Following is the outline of the play:

SAY:	DO:
1) *Sweep the parlor*	Brush your fingers lightly across the "wall" space between two corner jacks. (Catch the ball.)
2) *Sweep it clean*	Sweeping counterclockwise, brush your fingers lightly across the next "wall" space. (Catch the ball.)
3) *Leave no dust*	Brush your fingers lightly across the next "wall" space (counterclockwise). (Catch the ball.)

4) *To be seen*   Brush your fingers lightly across the last "wall" space. (Catch the ball.)

5) *Move a chair*   Push one of the corner jacks into the center. (Catch the ball.)

6) *Sweep it there*   Brush your fingers lightly across the space where the "chair" was. (Catch the ball.)

7) *Move a chair*   Push another corner jack into the center. (Catch the ball.)

8) *Sweep it there*   Brush your fingers lightly across the space where that "chair" was. (Catch the ball.)

9) *Move a chair*   Push another corner jack into the center. (Catch the ball.)

10) *Sweep it there*   Brush your fingers lightly across the space where that "chair" was. (Catch the ball.)

11) *Move a chair*   Push the last corner jack into the center. (Catch the ball.)

12) *Sweep it there*   Brush your fingers lightly across the space where the last "chair" was. (Catch the ball.)

13) *Pick up all the dust* Pick up all the jacks. (Catch the ball.)

If you move the wrong jack, say the wrong line, do the wrong action, or do not pick up all the jacks at the end, it counts as a miss.

When doing the multiples of Sweep the Parlor, do first two, then three, or even four of the above steps between the time you throw the ball up and the time you catch it. The chart for multiples of Sweep the Parlor looks like this:

	FIRST MOVE	SECOND MOVE	THIRD MOVE
DOUBLE:	1, 2	3, 4	5, 6
TRIPLE:	1, 2, 3	4, 5, 6	7, 8, 9
QUADRUPLE:	1, 2, 3, 4	5, 6, 7, 8	9, 10, 11, 12

	FOURTH MOVE	FIFTH MOVE
DOUBLE:	7, 8	9, 10
TRIPLE:	10, 11, 12	13, slap, slap
QUADRUPLE:	13, slap, slap, slap	

	SIXTH MOVE	SEVENTH MOVE
DOUBLE:	11, 12	13, slap
TRIPLE:		
QUADRUPLE:		

In Triple and Quadruple Sweep the Parlor, you will have to speak very fast, as well as do the actions quickly!

LEAD BALLOONS

Lead Balloons is an elaboration of *plainsies*. You do not use a ball; instead you use an extra jack to throw into the air. In this fancy, you must be very quick because a jack does not bounce! Follow the procedure for plainsies outlined in Chapter 2 (p. 10). However, instead of a ball, throw a jack into the air, pick up the jacks from the floor, and catch the falling jack *before* it hits the floor. It is often a good idea to throw the jack fairly high to allow yourself plenty of time to do the fancy.

You can make almost any fancy Lead Balloons. Just remember which jack is supposed to be the ball, especially if you must do a backward or forward flip.

BOUNCING BABIES

In this fancy, you pick up the jacks with one hand while you keep the "baby," the ball, bouncing with the other.

You cannot flip for Bouncing Babies. First throw out all the jacks. With your left hand, throw the ball up. With your right hand, pick up one jack. *Then* catch the ball with your left hand. Continue in this way, keeping the jacks you pick up in your right hand and the ball in your left, until all the jacks are picked up. Then throw them out and begin twosies.

Timing is important in this fancy. If you catch the ball before you pick up the jacks with your right hand, or if you pick up the jacks before you throw the ball up with your left hand, it counts as a miss.

II · Slams

SLAMS are fun to do after you have done six or seven
fancies. They are not very hard. However, if you miss on
a slam fancy, you must start all over again on plainsies!

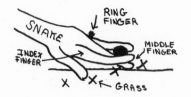

SNAKE-IN-THE-GRASS

Snake-in-the-Grass is a very easy fancy if you have a good hold on the ball—and if you don't talk!

Arrange the jacks in a straight line about two inches apart. Hold the ball atop your middle finger by slightly raising your index and ring fingers. As soon as the ball is in place, you may not talk until you are finished. Imagine that the jacks are numbered from 1 to 6 from left to right. Now move the tip of your middle finger (with the ball resting on it) among the jacks in the following pattern without lifting your finger from the floor.

Move (right) over *1*—under *2*—over *3*—under *4*—over *5*—under *6*—(move left) over *6, 5*—under *4, 3*—over *2, 1*—(right) under *1, 2, 3*—over *4, 5, 6*—(left) under *6, 5, 4, 3*—over *2, 1*—(right) under *1, 2, 3, 4, 5*—over *6* (left) under *6, 5, 4, 3, 2, 1*—(right) over *1, 2, 3, 4, 5, 6.*

At the end of this pattern, knock once at *1* and once at *6* with the tip of your middle finger. Throw the ball up from its held position, pick up all jacks, and catch the ball after one bounce. You are now finished and may talk.

If you lift the tip of your middle finger from the floor while moving during the pattern, if you touch or move a jack, if you forget the pattern, or if you talk, it counts as a miss and you start over again on plainsies. It is a lot of fun to try to make the other person talk!

BABIES

In Babies, you do not use the ball at all. Put it aside.

You cannot flip for Babies, and as soon as you throw all the jacks out, you may not talk until you have finished. Put the heel of your hand on the floor. You may not lift it off the floor until you are finished. With your right hand, pick up a jack, keep it in that hand, pick up another jack, keep it in your hand, and so on. When all the jacks have been picked up, throw them all out without lifting the heel of your hand from the floor, and begin twosies. Continue in this manner through sixies and then back again through onesies. At the end of onesies, you may talk and lift the heel of your hand from the floor.

If you move a jack, lift the heel of your hand from the floor, drop a jack that you have picked up, or talk, it counts as a miss. And a miss slams you back to the beginning again!

12 · Everlastings

Single Everlastings   Double Everlastings   Triple Everlastings
Quadruple Everlastings   Quintuple Everlastings
Sextuple Everlastings

EVERLASTINGS is the supreme ruler of all the fancies. If you can do a multiple of Everlastings well, you have mastered some of the most important principles of jacks. Furthermore, you have a trusty weapon to use against your opponents. The rhythm, the timing, the techniques, and the skills involved make the multiples of Everlastings exciting to watch and to play. Master Single Everlastings first. The *rules* and *techniques* for Single Everlastings apply to the Multiple Everlastings too.

Flipping: Never flip for any type of Everlastings.

Throwing out: Hold all six jacks in your right hand together with the ball. Throw the ball into the air, keeping the jacks in your hand. Then scatter the jacks on the floor and catch the ball before it bounces more than once. It is best to throw the ball fairly high so you will have ample time to use some of the throwing techniques described in Chapter 4 (p. 17). This is the way the jacks are thrown out *every* time. *Never* use your left hand in Everlastings.

Picking up: Throw the ball up, pick up a jack or a group of jacks just as you do in *plainsies* (Chapter 2), and catch the ball before it bounces more than once. The only difference here is that you keep the jacks you have picked up in your *right* hand. *Never* transfer them to your left hand or put them on the floor.

In Everlastings, unlike plainsies, you must go up to sixies, repeat sixies, and return to onesies again. For the most part, the "misses" are the same:

1. *Committing any of the ten basic fouls.* Any of the ten basic fouls described in Chapter 2 are misses.

2. *Throwing the jacks out without throwing the ball up.* If you throw the jacks out without throwing the ball up and catching it, it is a miss.

3. *Using your left hand.* From the beginning of Everlastings to the end, you *never* use your left hand for anything.

4. *Dropping a jack out of your hand.* If you have several jacks in your hand and are picking up another one, you may lose one of the jacks from your hand. This counts as a miss even if you pick it up again before catching the ball.

5. *Not using distinct, separate motions to pick up the jacks*

in Multiple Everlastings. In twosies Triple Everlastings, for example, you must pick up two jacks, then two more jacks, and finally two more jacks before catching the ball. If you pick up four, then two, or all six at once, it counts as a miss. The motions must be separate; you cannot mass all the jacks together and pick them up.

6. *Forgetting to slap a sufficient number of times.* If you forget to slap, or do not slap enough times, it is a miss.

None of the situations in *strictsies* and *funsies* described in Chapter 3 apply to Everlastings. Late Jack, Overs, Cracksies, Hands, Kissies, Haystacks, Carts, Touch-Me-Not, Split Jack, and Interference are completely disregarded. If any of these situations arise, they count as a miss, or you must play as well as possible without them. There are two kinds of Everlastings:

Eternal: If you miss on an Eternal Everlastings, you must start over again on onesies at the beginning of your next turn. Even if you miss on twosies coming back down from sixies, you must start on onesies going up on your next turn. You must do the whole Eternal Everlastings perfectly before you can leave it.

Noneternal: If you miss on Noneternal Everlastings, you can start from the place where you missed on your next turn. You do not have to go back to onesies.

Everlastings are always understood to be Eternal. You must specify in introducing the fancy if you want them to be Noneternal.

The multiples of Everlastings are just like all other multiple fancies. Follow the charts and pointers given in Chapter 5 (p. 24). If you can do Sextuple Everlastings, you are a champion!